FAILURE

IS ONLY A

BRUISE

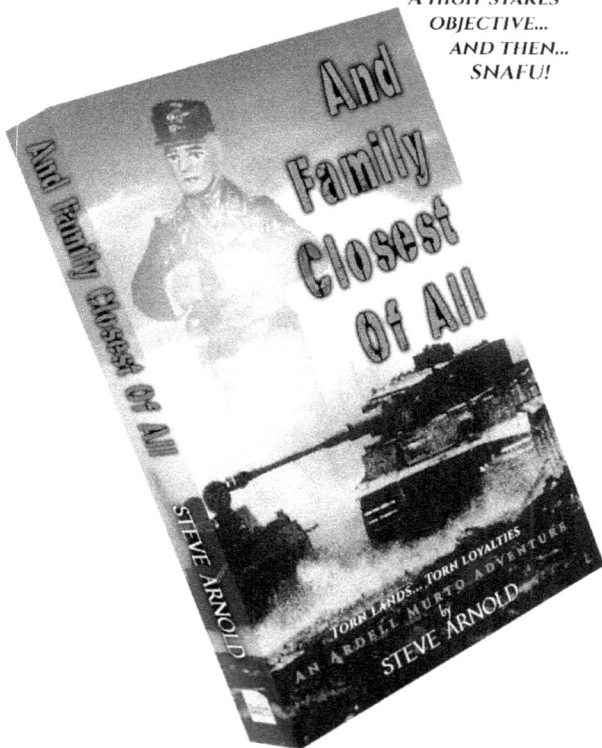

FAILURE

IS ONLY A

BRUISE

Lessons From When The Sky Fell

By

Steven Arnold MD

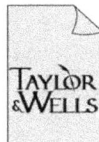

TAYLOR
&WELLS

Chardon, Ohio, USA

Taylor & Wells Publishing
11525 Taylor-Wells Rd.
Chardon, OH, USA 44024
www.taylor-wells.com

First Print Edition

Front and back cover art and all interior illustrations by the author,
with the exception of p. 80 and p. 103, which are public domain.

Printed in the United States of America

ISBN 979-8-9908505-4-5

FOR ANA,
WHO WAS THERE WHEN THE SKY FELL,
AND STAYED BEHIND TO PICK UP THE PIECES.

Table of Contents

Part Three: Coping

Preface

"All the darkness in the world cannot extinguish the light of a single candle."
—*St. Francis of Assisi*

Some years ago a very good friend of mine told me the sorry tale of a relative of his that had gone through a nasty, painful divorce. It had taken a toll on the poor guy (we'll call him 'Bob') and he had had all the trouble you can imagine dealing with it.

Then came the day that another guy in their church congregation (we'll call him 'George') found himself in the same boat. Their bishop felt he, himself, was out of his depth in trying to counsel George (having been happily married for many years) and turned to Bob to help guide George through what was going to be a horrendously difficult time. "I'm sorry to do this to you, Bob," offered the bishop, "because I know it's going to open up a lot of old wounds for you."

"It's okay," Bob reassured him. "You're right, it's going to hurt. It's going to hurt like hell.

"But if I don't help George, *then everything I went through was for nothing.*"

That, in a nutshell, is the reason for this book.

Part One:
Dealing
With Doctors

What the heck are they even thinking?

SJA'24

Keep It Together!

"Documentation is a love letter that you write to your future self."

—*Damian Conway*

I've served in two branches of the U.S. military: first in the Army, as a cavalry scout (which paid for college) and then in the Navy, as a physician. One lesson I learned early on was:

Always keep your medical records with you!

This makes sense in the military. Station changes are common, and your files won't always arrive when you do. And even though we had an electronic medical records system (EMR), it often crashed, usually about 5pm Eastern time, when all the major facilities on the East Coast weretrying to finish their charting and go home! It also had some odd quirks to it – as a doctor in Twentynine Palms I found I could easily pull up records from Guam or Okinawa, but getting anything from San Diego, only three hours away, seemed beyond the pale.

In the Army, at least, we were required to have hard copies of our records always ready to hand, and had to bring them in to our battalion physicals for review. I never saw my First Sergeant cry until he showed up one year without his records and got to the vaccine station. The medic asked for his records, Top said he forgot them at home, and the medic just shook his head and started laying out one vaccine syringe after another. Top asked him what he was doing, and the medic calmly replied, "Without proof of your shot record, I have to *give* you all your shots today." And there's a lot in the Army.

As a physician in civilian life, I am often confidently told by my patients their files from another hospital are "all on your computer there," to which I've had to explain, much to their surprise, that they aren't.

The fact is that each hospital system has their own EMR. Granted there are some major platforms that are popular with several systems, like Epic and Athena, but even though two hospital groups may use the same platform, each one maintains their own files *separate* from everyone else's. Cleveland Clinic does not share its records with the Mayo Clinic, and so forth.

The reason for this is related to the ownership of those records. 'So *who* owns my records?' you may ask.

The general rule is that the records belong to the entity that created them. This goes back to copyright law of intellectual property. If your doctor is employed by a group or hospital system, the employer claims ownership rather than the physician (unless they have a contract to the contrary). This actually makes sense: if your doctor decides to move to another area, but you plan on staying at the same clinic and just following up with the new provider, all your records are still at that clinic. The hospital acts as a steward of your records and will not release them to another party without your written permission – even if that other party is yourself!

This usually isn't a huge problem. These hospitals aren't trying to hold your records hostage, they just want to respect the law. But it does involve an extra step to get your hands on them, and these entities are allowed to charge for copies and postage if you want them printed out for you. And it can take time to get them – a *lot* of time. Waiting for weeks, or even months, is not unheard of.

This becomes really important when a malpractice case comes up. Having to wait for records <u>will</u> delay preparation. Sometimes records arrive in bits and pieces, some from here, some from there, and sometimes a facility won't send everything all at once, for whatever reason. You might miss a statute of limitations deadline waiting for records. You might spend a lot of money thinking you have a case, only to find out at the eleventh hour that you don't have the documentation to make it.

So what do you do?

Keep files as you go! Get copies of visit notes after you've seen your doctor, or have been to the hospital, or at regular intervals if you have a family member in a nursing home. And if you're not good at organizing, don't worry. Sorting the records can be confusing and that's what your legal team and I (your consultant) are here for. To be honest, you and I may have different ideas of how to organize records and that can make important details *harder* for me to find. Your best bet is to just put everything in chronological order.

But be aware that the 'After Visit Summary' you get from your PCP, or the 'Patient Discharge Instructions' you get as you leave the hospital, are the barest surface of what was done. It's only the info you as a patient need to know (it's kind of like that old military idea of information being given on a 'need to know basis'). Behind those documents are pages (sometimes hundreds) of labs, progress notes, imaging reports, assessments and other records that tell the actual story of <u>what</u> happened, and more importantly, *why*. This won't be given to you unless you ask for them (with that signed release) and these are the records that you need to have with you. These are the records that give me, as your consultant, an insight into what your doctors were thinking, the information they had available, when they had it, and what influenced their decisions.

With a current file of your records in hand you will be better prepared to handle any adverse events. It's also not a bad idea to have even for something as simple as *you* moving to another area. Remember, sometimes it can take weeks for a hospital to respond to a records request, and you may need to see your new doctor before then. So keep it together!

Ugh. Jargon...

"Jargon is part ceremonial robe, part false beard."

—*Mason Cooley*

In 1910 a gent by the name of Silvanus P. Thompson published a book with the surprising title of 'Calculus Made Easy'. It was the apparent audacity of that appellation that caught my eye decades later, and I bought it in the hopes it would live up to its own hype.

Much to my elated surprise it did. Turns out the esteemed Professor Thompson had been a physics lecturer at the City and Guilds Technical College in Finsbury, England, and had a refreshingly low opinion of math teachers in general. This was one of the things that endeared me to him – well, that and the fact that he actually *was* able to explain calculus in straightforward, layman's terms so it made sense. But at the very outset he lamented overstuffed professors that seemed to work at making math harder than it really needed to be, apparently just to make themselves look smart, or at least important.

That was something I could really sympathize with, being a math major in college. I had one professor in particular in my freshman year who had a bad habit of obfuscating his calculus in layers of sophisticated algebra. Mind you, you do need to know a little algebra to work calculus, but you generally only need the most basic forms. You don't even need quadratic formula-level equational gymnastics to make derivates dance for you. What having a ready skill with algebra *does* do in calculus, is allow you to take shortcuts so you don't have to work so long to find the solution. That's great if you're in a hurry, or maybe lazy, but when you're trying to *teach* how calculus works it doesn't do anything for you to lose your pupils in the weeds of your algebra before you even get to an integral sign. To be honest, if I hadn't had Mr. Thompson's book I would have been completely lost and by the time I was done with that class I felt like I had paid my tuition for the privilege of figuring it out for myself.

At the other end of the spectrum was my high school trigonometry teacher, Mrs. Rozycki. She was someone Mr. Thompson would have liked, I think. She taught us a silly little rhyme (that I recall to this day) to remember the basic forms of the sine, cosine and tangent equations. The neat thing about trigonometry is that if you know those three, you can figure out all the rest with a little very basic algebra and a couple extra steps. Sure, it takes longer. By like thirty seconds. But I would have lost so much more time trying to decide which of the myriad permutations of those equations I would need to solve any problem, using that rhyme was like taking a switchback trail so I wouldn't have to climb straight up a cliff. More distance, but way less time and effort (and risk of mishap).

All this leads me to medical jargon. One of the things I've encountered in my consulting work is that I do a fair amount of explaining what the terminology means. This isn't a problem for me, and I don't think less of ordinary folks or legal professionals because they don't happen to know the difference between *hypo* and *hyper*. I wouldn't expect them to. Seriously, I had no real grasp of *ex parte* or what a *jurat* was until I started doing consulting, and those terms are just as Latin as *flexor hallucis longus*. My criticism is toward the doctors that throw around medical terminology with little apparent regard to the people to whom they're speaking. Doctors like Mr. Thompson's math professors.

Why are some doctors like this? All I can tell you is that doctors are people like everyone else, and *there are all kinds*. Some just get in the habit of speaking in such a way among their peers and they have difficulty switching gears when talking to the general public. Some really don't seem to notice that the jargon is too esoteric for their audience. And yes, there are those that just want to show off.

I'm not talking about things written in the medical record. Those are internal documents, written by doctors for doctors. We know what we're saying and we *are* in a hurry and the shorthand helps us get home in time for dinner. But it really gets under my skin when a doctor is talking to a patient or family member, in the moment, describing what's happening and what their plan is, and they're throwing around a lot of lingo that clearly is going right over the recipient's head with no hope of landing. More than once has a friend or family member come to me afterward to have me explain what this or that meant. It's unfortunate that they felt they had to handle things that way because now they've missed an opportunity to ask clarifying questions of the doc that's got the life of their loved one in their hands. Sometimes we don't get a chance to go back and ask. Sometimes things just happen too fast.

One of the basic principles of medical care is that the patient has autonomy: that they can choose for themselves what is to be done to them. This requires informed consent. Informed consent requires you as a patient (or power of attorney) to understand what is happening and what is being offered, and *this* requires the physician to clearly present that information. On your level.

This is an important point: it is *incumbent upon the physician* to explain things in terms you can understand. It is incumbent upon you, on the other hand, to ask for clarification right then and there if there's something you don't get. You may *not* have another chance. And don't think you can just google it later. Just because you can find a definition doesn't mean you can fully grasp how it all fits into the big picture (see the chapter on "It's Not Always What You Think"). It's the doc's job to explain that.

And by the way, if you are struggling with calculus, I highly recommend Mr. Thompson's book. It's on Amazon and it's less than twenty bucks.

Radiology Scrabble! MRI, CT, US?

"Never be so focused on what you're look-
ing for that you overlook the thing you
actually find."

—*Ann Patchett*

I grew up watching the original *Star Trek* – the one with Bill Shatner & Co. At the time I thought it was pretty cool that Dr. McCoy had that little hand-held scanner gizmo that could tell him exactly what was going wrong with the guy that had just been beamed through a wall. Since then, the idea of a 'whole-body' scanner has been a staple of future fiction and has left a lot of us wondering when we're actually going to have something like that?

The fact of the matter is, probably not for a while. There are actually some really sound reasons that we have so many imaging modalities: first, they don't all look at the same thing. It's really like using the right tool for the job. Then there are the side effects, and finally costs also can vary widely and, let's face it, there's just no reason to spend more than you need (I can already hear the gasps from the Medical-Industrial-Political Machine).

In clinical practice I've often come across a misconception that there is some kind of progression of 'betterness' among the different systems: X-rays aren't as good as ultrasounds which aren't as good as CTs which aren't as good as MRIs. In reality they all have their strengths and weaknesses. Ultrasounds are good for soft tissues and are easy to use in real time, and side effects are nil. MRIs are also good for soft tissues but are not an 'as it's happening' imaging system and are *a lot* more expensive, but the level of detail is much better. X-rays are good for looking at more solid structures like bones and kidney stones, and with the addition of radio-opaque markers are quick and easy for things like pulmonary emboli, when a person's life can be hanging in the balance. CTs are really just fancy X-rays, taken from multiple angles, so the cost is naturally higher simply because more images are being taken, but these can be used to reconstruct three dimensional structures.

There are also limitations based on the systems' physics: MRIs use powerful magnetic fields and can rip a steel implant right out of you (this is why surgical hardware is usually made of titanium). X-rays and CTs use radiation which must be carefully limited (which is one reason why many times an X-ray on a child will *not* be ordered: there's no need to start irradiating them early, they'll get plenty of that when they're 80).

These are the reasons I don't feel we're going to see some kind of 'all-in-one' scanner widget any time soon, at least not with our current technology: we'd have to combine these all into one device and then that 26-week fetus would get a dose of radiation more suited to a pneumonia patient, while zinging her mom's navel piercing across the room like a bullet. And then charge her for it!

So how does the doctor decide what to order? It's something of an art form, actually, and from my standpoint, if I don't know right off the top of my head it's always a good idea to talk to the radiologist. I would tell them what I thought I was looking for and they would recommend the best imaging. This may sound a little backward, since one might assume we order scans to see what *is* wrong, but the actual process is to try to figure out what you are dealing with first (which is why we ask a hundred questions right off the bat, and then start poking and prodding), and *then* order a scan that will either confirm or deny it (take a look at the chapter "Smoking Gun? Or Red Herring?"). And sometimes the educated guess isn't right anyway, and you find something unexpected that would have shown up better on a different scan. This is why you sometimes get wording in the report to the effect that, 'a CT with contrast would have been a lot cooler'.

There are whole books written on when and where and why to use this method over that one. Just so we in the trenches can sort it out with a lot less trouble, most of us have found some handy reference (read that 'cheat-sheet') that's not so voluminous. And then, of course, there's an entire medical specialty dedicated to just that task!

This page intentionally left blank

How Much Do Doctors Really Know?

"Real knowledge is to know the extent of one's ignorance."

—*Confucius*

How much *do* doctors know? The short answer is, a lot, if it's about something they deal with every day. Or something they've personally encountered, or suffered from, or otherwise have a passion about (for example, my professor on ankylosing spondylitis, actually *had* ankylosing spondylitis). So, count one passion, a few health events in their immediate circle, and a few dozen common ailments in their specialty.

Aside from these, there's going to be a varying amount of readily-available data in your physician's mental rolodex, and it's going to vary from doctor to doctor. To understand why that is, let's have a look at the process of medical education, at least where I went to school:

I spent the first year of my medical education learning how things are supposed to work: the functioning of a normal healthy body. The second year was focused on the ways things can go wrong. Keep in mind, there are *tens of thousands* of ways things can go wrong, so conditions that were studied were chosen partly due to being common, and partly due to being very illustrative of particular abnormal processes (I think this is why every licensing exam seemed to have questions about pheochromocytomas, despite the fact that anyone besides an endocrinologist would be lucky to actually see one even once in their lifetime).

The next two years were spent doing clinical rotations. Every month we would do time in a different specialty, this month orthopedics, next month dermatology, then neurosurgery – you get the idea. What you would learn there was *very* highly dependent on what cases happened to come in during the time you were on service. Granted the attending physicians would give us assignments to research and report on, to teach us things that didn't come up during our rotation, but the stuff that would really stick with you was the stuff you actually *saw*.

Then comes residency – on the job training in one's chosen specialty. For Family Practice, it's a lot like med school, a different service every month, because we're generalists and need to know something about *everything*. (As a matter of fact, a couple years after graduation I ran into a former classmate. If I recall correctly, she had gone into Hematology. In any case she admitted she had initially thought about going into Family Practice but in the end had decided that field just had 'too much to know'!)

Then you get out into clinical practice and start seeing what's really out there. You get good at the stuff you see every day, of course, but I for one am glad I found myself practicing in rural areas, where I saw off-the-wall conditions not seen elsewhere, just because I was the only ready resource around.

Now the key point here is, what about the odd stuff? Everyone has seen movies where a doctor is confronted with something really weird and they have to hit the lab. In reality not all of us are skilled researchers and most of us don't have a lab to go to, or the time to spend in it, but it makes a convenient plot shortcut for a screenwriter (plus it looks cool). The important thing is that they know that they don't know, but they also know they need to find out – and how to do that.

After I had been in the Army for a few years I was shipped off to the Primary Leadership Development School. This was the first step in education for non-commissioned officers and I was a little surprised to find that all the tests were open-book. This might tempt some to crack jokes about the average intelligence level of an NCO, but let me tell you that among the thirty or so guys in my scout platoon in the Guard, we had an IT engineer, a high-school math teacher, a high-school principal, a pre-law student, a police officer, and me, who was pre-med. The tests were open book because the cadre were reinforcing the point that you weren't expected to know everything, but *you were supposed to know where to find it.*

That's an attitude that has carried me through a lot of my practice. It's impossible to know everything there is to know. There are literally thousands of research papers published every year. Let's face it, a century and a half ago medical knowledge was a lot more scant (there's a meme going around about how back then a woman seeking treatment for depression was liable to get a dose of cocaine and a session with a vibrator, and there's a certain amount of truth to that!). A smart doc knows the limits of their knowledge and has the references to look things up when they reach that boundary. One of the things I was taught was that, if you were stepping into the exam room to have a look at something you weren't familiar with, you first took a few minutes to review your sources and have a quick brush-up. This isn't a sign of intellectual deficiency. It's an honest understanding of one's own shortcomings and a willingness to work to overcome them. We were taught enough to function, and we were then taught to *learn from our patients*. And keep your books handy!

So don't be dismayed if your doctor gets that momentary look of confusion on their face when you tell them something. You only need to be dismayed if they don't do something about it.

Death Certificates – How Accurate Are They, Really?

"Accuracy and clarity of statement are mutually exclusive."

—*Niels Bohr*

The answer to this is, like so many other things in life, is that... it depends.

The actual process of filling out a death certificate is a team effort: the family usually provides the information about birthdates, birthplaces, parents, and so forth; the funeral director handles the time and place of death; but it's up to the doctor to fill out the actual cause, and this is the part that is of the most interest, and subject to the widest interpretation.

On the one hand, a death certificate is one of what we call 'vital records', a document recording important facts about a person. As such we try to make sure they are as accurate as possible.

On the other hand, there is a lot of pressure to get them done quickly. Usually, a funeral home needs a completed death certificate before they can make a final disposition of the deceased person. The doctors completing them don't want to let them go unfinished for too long because one's memory of what happened at the very end can get distorted. And families generally want to get their loved one's affairs settled and have some closure.

This doesn't mean we try to get them done on a rush basis. It isn't a 'just put something in there and move on to the next case' kind of thing. It's a matter of how much is known, and when did the doctor know it?

When I was a med student I did a month with the neurosurgery team at MetroHealth in Cleveland. One of my attending physicians made an observation that has stuck with me through the years: "As doctors," Dr. Likavec cautioned, "we are often called upon to make decisions based on incomplete information." I have found this was never more true than in the death certificate. I've completed my fair share over the years, and sometimes even despite knowing my patients very well, those final days or hours can take some unexpected turns. Sometimes you know all the facts and it's straightforward. But sometimes listing the cause of death can be little more than a 'best guess' because definitive information just isn't available. Maybe the person wasn't actually under their regular doctor's care at the very end – they may have been in the emergency room, or transferred to an outside hospital, or at home, and whatever records there may be (if any even exist) may take days or weeks to collect. For myself, at such times I would try to defer the task to the ED doctor/hospitalist/hospice staff because they were actually there and saw what happened (and would have the records). Sometimes I would have the chance to talk to them myself and get the story. And sometimes I would just have to make the best assessment I could with the information I had. I always tried to be accurate, but there can be obstacles that can be hard to overcome in a timely fashion.

"What about an autopsy?" you may ask. While these are pretty much the gold standard when it comes to cause of death, they are only carried out in specific circumstances (see your state's laws for particulars) and the vast majority of times, won't be done (unless you want to pay for it).

On a side note, a few years ago during the pandemic, there was a lot of talk about death certificates having 'COVID-19' listed as a cause of death when it shouldn't have been. I can say from the perspective of a physician that, any doctor filling out a death certificate knows it's their signature, and their license, on the line – literally. There is no place to list who they worked for or whatever pressures they may have felt from higher-ups to put something down as a cause. To write something knowingly false on a vital record is illegal but you can't just blame that on your hospital CEO.

But keep in mind that the death certificate lists an 'immediate cause of death' and then leaves space for a number of possible 'contributing factors', and sometimes these are the diagnoses that we suspect but lack concrete evidence for. Also keep in mind that, at the time, we didn't know a lot about COVID-19, didn't have a good test for it, and often it may have been listed because it was *suspected* to *possibly* have been a factor.

On the other hand, I've dealt with enough hospital administrators to know that they can put real pressure on a doctor, and when the federal government is earmarking funds to deal with the fallout of a health crisis, there's an awful lot of incentive to list something as a 'contributing cause' with only the barest of connections.

What this all means is that the causes of death listed on a death certificate are not etched in stone. It may be a good, solid assessment, or it may be only a guess hampered by a lack of information. Only a thorough review of the records, and a knowledge of the person's health, can really sort out what actually happened at the end.

SJA '24

It's Not Always What You Think

"You must never assume! Because when you assume, you make an 'ASS' out of 'U' and 'ME'!"

—*Benny Hill*

If I've heard it once, I've heard it a thousand times: "That guy in room 203 has... (fill in with your favorite disease). It's obvious. I don't know why no one else sees it." Statements like this have been uttered with supreme confidence by everyone from non-medical lay people to registered nurses to med students, usually when the doctor treating 'that guy in 203' seems to go off into some diagnostic hinterland and everyone else is left shaking their head trying to figure out where the Good Doctor took a wrong turn.

This divergence of opinion usually arises when the statement-maker falls into the trap of thinking that, just because it looks like a duck, and quacks like a duck, it must be, in fact, a duck. When they take a collection of symptoms and fit them into a familiar pattern, which then becomes Fact. But this thinking is flawed, and is very closely related to a game I like to call...

"How many clicks on WebMD does it take before I have terminal cancer?"

The root of this problem is that symptoms are only the outward appearance of a problem – and any one symptom can arise due to a host of problems. Got a cough? Is it asthma or allergies? A cold, or COVID? Or even acid reflux? Got a pain in your knee? Crick in your neck? Or abdominal pain, which has literally dozens, if not hundreds, of causes? When you try to diagnose by clicking off a list of symptoms you're only doing half the work, and fitting those only to patterns you've seen before ("I knew someone once who looked just like that...") limits your options even further. Then a worried sufferer takes this to the internet, where the site host is trying desperately to avoid any legal liability and gives the worst news first, just to inspire their visitor to get to a real doctor... because it may actually not be a duck, it might be a mockingbird. Or even a parrot.

There's a natural tendency to do things this way. If we've seen it before, we probably have an idea of how to deal with it. That feels safe. The unknown is frightening, and the stakes are higher when we are looking after the welfare of another. And let's face it, 'common things are common because they are common'. But as a physician, we can't rely just on that. We have to be as sure, as we possibly and practically can be, of what we're dealing with. This means we also have to know *why it isn't what it looks like.*

I majored in Mathematics for my undergrad degree. I did that because I was good at it and I knew it would keep my grades up. I was surprised to find it had an unexpected benefit: the problem-solving skills I learned in dealing with the theories behind algebra and calculus really came into play when sorting out what's happening with my patients.

The basic attitude in mathematical theory is that no one thing is accepted as a true explanation of a phenomenon unless it can be *proven* that *nothing else* can explain it. In other words, it's not enough to find an explanation that *can* cause what you're seeing, you need to think of *everything else* that could look the same, and start ruling things out. In medicine this is when the lab tests, the imaging, the focused physical exam and the oddball questions about recent vacations in the tropics come in.

Now in math, we deal in absolutes, and there are very, very few absolutes in medicine. But the principles hold true. As a doctor, you're calling the shots. You're pointing the team in the direction they need to go. You have to be sure, as much as you can be given limitations of time and information, where that is, so you can successfully treat your patients. This means it is absolutely essential you not only know what it is, and why, *but what it isn't, and why*. And sometimes you find to your surprise that it really is a parrot. As a med student I was cautioned (very strongly) about the dangers of thinking you knew what was happening before you even walked into the room to see the patient. It's too easy to get tunnel vision when you're starting off with a preconceived notion, and that's a very good way to screw up. The fact this was drummed into us means even among doctors this tendency is all too common. And if that's all we're going to do as physicians then we may as well hang up our stethoscopes and let WebMD handle it.

This page accidentally left blank

Smoking Gun? Or Red Herring?

"Any fool can know. The point is to understand."

—*Albert Einstein*

As a family practice physician, I feel that giving patients access to their records via online patient portals has been a mixed blessing. On the one hand I've always been a big fan of folks having their records (see the chapter "Keep It Together!"). On the other, understanding what those reports and results mean is an entirely different animal. People try to do it themselves, and God bless them for it, because I think they should be actively engaged in their health. But those records are just put out there with essentially no context and that can lead to a lot of misunderstandings.

I'm not criticizing that lack of context, mind you. It takes a fair amount of time to explain what everything means and the typical workflow in a primary care clinic just won't allow that outside of an actual visit. It's just the nature of the beast. But getting into your doctor's office so they can take that time and do that explaining, means time off work, transportation, babysitting, copays, and (to channel my inner Yul Brenner), 'etcetera, etcetera, etcetera'. So people turn to Doctor Google and, quite often, end up more confused than when they started.

Add to that the fact that every lab has their own range of 'normal values' for any given result, and every radiologist seems to have their own favorite stock phrases they like to use when describing xrays and CT scans, and you have a recipe for absolute mayhem.

There's not enough room in a blog post to help people figure all these things out. That's literally why we spend four years in medical school followed up with anywhere from three to five years in residency. But what I can do, is go over some of the reasons *why* things are ordered. Maybe this will help folks understand why a result out of range is not necessarily a smoking gun (though it can be!).

First things first: why are some tests ordered, and others aren't? Or, even more baffling, why are they ordered in some cases of a particular condition and not in others? The rationale is, *a test is only ordered if the result is going to change the management.* If you're trying to distinguish a sprain that will get an ace wrap from a fracture that will get a cast, you *need* that xray. But if that sore throat has been going on for a week and it's only getting worse, and there's goop draining out of the tonsils, you're going to start antibiotics and worry about getting a culture later, if at all. This gatekeeping is done because any test has a certain margin of error and you may get something that looks off when it isn't. Not only that but, if you order something unnecessary and it comes back abnormal, you have to take time, resources and attention to do something with that – which may not be appropriate, and may even send you barking up the wrong tree.

Another problem with interpreting results is that quite often one abnormal result only means something if there's another result that is *also* abnormal... or maybe if a certain other *is* normal. There's a lot of interrelation between results. Then factor in anatomic variations, the reality that different people can react in completely opposite ways to the same treatments, *etcetera, etcetera, etcetera...*

and you see why context is *always* important. As doctors we are taught to 'treat the patient, not the numbers'. This means that the whole is more than just the sum of the parts. Getting the complete story is essential (which conversely means if the doctors aren't trying to get that story they're not doing their job).

There is a reason it's called the *art* of medicine. It's not a math problem (which is ironic, considering my background) (and never mind the Internal Medicine guys that have a formula for *everything*). So don't be confused, if it confuses you! We have to work pretty hard to figure it out sometimes, too.

This page... I don't know what happened to this page

So You're Considering
Medical School...

"I still say, 'Shoot for the Moon; you might get there.'"

—*Buzz Aldrin*

Everyone knows med school is hard. The difficulty is almost legendary, and to a certain extent, for good reason. But this has led, I feel, to unrealistic expectations among the general public about what it really takes to graduate, like everyone with a white coat and a stethoscope by default has to have an IQ of at least 140. This can be good or bad, I suppose, but I worry that people assume doctors have superhuman intellects and that can lead to all sorts of trouble. This is something I want to talk about because it really isn't like that. I especially want to show folks that, if becoming a doctor something you've thought about, you needn't be afraid of the process.

Besides that there are some of the everyday aspects of the culture of med school that most people don't think about. I had a lot of years under my belt working in blue-collar jobs before I got the idea in my head to go for broke. Not only that but everyone else in my family had done the same (working blue-collar, I mean), all farmers and carpenters for generations back. Not to disparage any of my ancestors! I used to joke that my grandfather, a dairy and chicken farmer, had tried to teach me to make things grow, and the best I could do was try to keep them alive! But when I finally got to med school I found that there were a lot of little things that everyone else in class seemed to know that I didn't (like the difference between an intern, a resident, and an attending).

And finally, I want to spell out the process plainly just for the sake of those who are curious. So here we go:

You start off in college. (I'm going to avoid programs like the Northeast Ohio Universities College Of Medicine that has a combined BS/MD program). Four years, you need. Pretty simple, right?

But what major? When I went to KSU, 'pre-med' was absolutely *not* a major: the idea was you were going to get a degree in something you could do if you didn't get into med school. That's not bad counsel, either. For my admitting class at Case there were 3,500 applicants for 140 seats and I didn't get in the first time I applied. So your back-up plan should be... what? Most people will tell you either Biology or Chemistry. I suppose that's fine if you like those fields, but I'm going to tell you something different: the most important thing about choosing your major is, *pick something you're good at.* Period. Med school will teach you everything you need to know to be a physician. What *they* want to know is, can you manage to complete a challenging curriculum, and excel at it? So a BA in General Studies with a 2.5 GPA probably won't cut it. You want something difficult in which you can shine, and you most definitely will need to get those stellar grades no matter what. So set yourself up for success and pick a field that suits you. When I did make it to Case, about half of our people were Bio & Chem majors, but the rest were pretty much everything else you could imagine: we had a music teacher, at least one MBA, a pre-law guy that changed his mind, and me, with a degree in mathematics.

That mathematics degree... that's a story all by itself. In my naivete when I enrolled at Kent, I listed Pre-Med as my major. It didn't take long for the admissions dean to call me into his office to explain (very nicely) the point I made above. I needed a real major. What would he suggest, I asked? He said most people pick Bio or Chem, for obvious reasons. Now, my thinking was, what's a Bio degree going to do for me if I don't get into med school? Get me a job as a lab tech? I'd make less than I was in the factory. A Biology Teacher? Umm... just no, definitely not something I have the temperament for. So that was out. And Chemistry? I lived in Northeast Ohio, the polymer capital of the world. The Goodyear Blimp hangar was only an hour away. Getting a chem degree around here pretty much guaranteed a job as Plant Chemist, and I wasn't going back to the factory, those guys spent almost as much time on the floor as I had.

What about math? I asked. He looked a little dumbfounded and said he'd have to ask his supervisor but in the end it was approved. Good thing, too. I figured out that what math does, really, is *train your brain to solve problems logically,* and that discipline has been a real boon when it comes to diagnosing an illness. It's a lot like solving a math proof: What information am I given, what can I deduce from that information, and what more do I need to determine?

The next step is to take the MCAT, the Medical College Admissions Test. It's like the SATs for med school. There are whole books and courses written about preparing for that so I'm only going to mention it here as the next step.

Then you apply to med school and go through the whole interview process. Again, reams printed on this. It's pretty much everything you can expect.

Then you're in! And it's nose-to-the-grindstone and everyone starts showing you their rashes and asking you uncomfortably personal questions about their bowel movements like you're already reassembling cadavers in your basement and winching them up to the thundering sky. Get used to that. (Folks mean well but they don't realize that you aren't going to be able to afford an Eastern European castle with a lab fully decked out like a steampunk rave until you're well into your years as an attending). The medical education you get is going to be general. You'll get something of everything. Think of it like high school: there, you had to take a lot of classes in things that you probably would never use because they needed to prepare you for *any* subsequent training you may take, be it college, technical school, or just striking out on your own. Med school is the same way.

Generally, as you get close to graduation, you apply to a residency program (I'm skipping over the Step Exams, because again, volumes have already been written and they change the format every so often – but you do need to get these done before graduation). Residency is your on-the-job training in your chosen specialty. It's like going to college after high school and choosing that major. There *are* doctors that go out into practice without residency, but it's hard to get licensed that way, if not impossible. In any case, now you're getting paid. It's not a staggering amount (I'd say a little more than what I would have been making in the factory if I had stayed) but at least you're not adding to your student loan balance. There's this thing called Match Day that you may hear people a-buzz about. That's because all the residencies in the country put all their open positions into one database, and all the graduates put their druthers in as well, and then they're matched up and you find out where you're going. It all happens at one time.

Once you're in residency things get real. Now you are a physician. You've graduated. Your signature means something. You are a doctor in every sense of the word. Granted, you're fresh out of the wrapper, as it were, and you literally know just enough to be dangerous, so you're still working under supervision, but you've got those letters after your name. First year is called your 'intern' year. All years after that (residency lengths vary by specialty, and last from 3 to 5 years) you're a 'resident' (from when student doctors used to live at the hospitals – which it still feels like, some days). Once you finish residency you can, if you enjoy the punishment, do some optional training in a subspeciality called a 'fellowship', and after that you are done and you have attained the lofty title of 'attending physician'.

That covers the vast majority of medical education programs. Just don't ask the maxillofacial surgeons what they went through unless you packed a lunch. And probably a second breakfast. Honestly, props to those folks.

How do you excel through all this? Without that IQ of 140 (or even with it?). Of course, you need to have a good work ethic, be punctual, and get along well with others (I guess unless you're a pathologist or a radiologist – just kidding!) and you do have to know a fair amount of things, there's just no way around that (although a neurosurgeon I worked with once pointed out with no sarcasm at all that he knew how to do four operations – that was it, and was all he needed. He was fascinated that I was going into Family Practice). But you don't have to have everything memorized, you just need to know how to find it when you need it. But the best advice I can give you is *be organized.* One of my colleagues in residency was really bright and really nice, but he just couldn't seem to get his ideas grouped and correlated. Doctors are *busy* and lives are in the balance. We need to be able to communicate clearly and succinctly and get salient points across fast without a lot of fluff and bother. He was the only doc I ever saw let go after only an intern year. That's right, they didn't renew his contract for the balance of residency. And it was the poor organizational skills that did him in.

I hope this takes some of the mystery out of the process of becoming a doctor, and maybe inspires some of you to take the dive.

Part Two:
The Medical-
Industrial-Political
Machine

Military-Industrial Complex?
So Twentieth Century!

SJA '24

Who Runs The Hospitals?

"Pay no attention to the man behind the curtain!"'

—*Oz the Great
and Terrible*

Steward Medical Group is folding like it's laundry day. This is one of those news noshes that initially surprised me, but then, really didn't. I used to work for Steward a few years ago, when they expanded out of Connecticut by buying a handful of hospitals in Ohio including the one I worked for. The surprise was when I recognized their name in the news. The not-surprise came as I read about the details of why SMG was having money troubles: corporate types were putting short-term profitability over patient care and looking after their staff? Yeah, that sounded familiar. Probably a good thing for me in the long run that the pandemic made SMG close down my clinic and cut me loose.

But looking at their money woes brings to light a topic I've been pondering writing on for some time: Who really does run the hospitals? Now I'm talking about the big multi-facility organizations like SMG. Or Community Health Systems, or Cleveland Clinic. I'm sure everyone knows there are MBA's in the upper echelons, but it may surprise folks to find out that the doctors definitely do *not* run the show.

Most hospitals are businesses. Even the non-profit ones – the only difference is what happens to any excess funds. But doctors, by and large, are businessmen only secondarily, and they usually don't have the skills to run a large health care system. Especially when the money isn't coming in directly from patients in a cash-on-the-barrel-head arrangement but by circuitous routes from private and government insurers who require copays and pre-authorizations, and local, state and federal incentive programs to promote one politicized health goal or another. This can be further complicated by the new 'Accountable Care Organization' payment models initially adopted by groups like Steward and now becoming part of the Medicaid/Medicare landscape. In these models, money is allotted in an insurer's budget for each of their patients, depending on their specific mix of diagnoses in a kind of 'worst case scenario, this is what we'll spend' projection. Then, if that patient's budget is not spent (meaning they were kept healthier than expected) the saved money is split between the insurer and the patient's care team at some agreed-upon percentage. This isn't a bad idea on the face of it, because it incentivizes preventative health measures, and that old adage about an ounce of prevention is very true. ACO's actually pay hospital systems to take care of folks in the clinics and keep them out of the inpatient floors. But even from its early days back in the mid 2010's I worried about the long-term sustainability of such a model: as years go by and the system works, people theoretically become healthier and their required budgets naturally shrink, which means it gets harder and harder to save any money, until the hospital is just breaking even... if that. And then they close Northside in Youngstown entirely.

So the top tier of decision makers are MBA's. With all the money coming in from insurers, Medicaid, Aetna et al. also have a really strong (if not necessarily direct) say in operations. And government money *always* has strings attached. Not that those strings aren't justified (the government is spending our money after all), but it does mean they have their finger in the pie right along with everyone else. The doctors are there, somewhere, but not where their hands are on the purse strings. Just look up the organizational chart for your favorite facility: there's usually a 'Medical Director'. They're the doctor in charge of other doctors, but the doctors are really little more than highly-trained production workers, making the medical director a shift foreman (I can't even say he's a union boss – though sometimes the nurses and support staff have those). Doctors see the people whose insurers pay the bills. It's almost like we're the exotic dancers at the strip club – we have a skill people pay to avail themselves of. We can complain about how the way things are done impact care, but it's up to the hospital leadership to decide if they want to listen. And quite often the suit-and-tie gang have their own ideas.

As a matter of fact, it was one of Steward's hallmarks that impressed me the most when they bought my hospital, that they actually *were* run by doctors. But then I guess their current state tells you how *that* worked out.

If you have a hard time visualizing doctors as line workers (or exotic dancers for that matter), let me tell you how the hospitals were staffed in the Navy: All leadership positions were Medical Service Corps (i.e., RNs and the like), not Medical Corps. The hospital CO, XO, and each department chief. The doctors were needed to see patients, so the admin jobs were MSC officers. We were really in the trenches, not for the same reason at the top end as civilian hospitals, but for the same reason on our end. We had to make things happen in a very real sense.

The answer to the question of who runs hospitals, really, is pretty much everyone *except* the doctors. It's the folks with the money, just like everywhere else. And lest you think letting the government run them is the solution, let me just point out that they're the biggest offenders of all. I don't have a good solution to this, not yet. But my basic stance on pretty much everything has always been decentralization of power. But I'll have to address that on another day.

Healthcare Hostages

"Heck. What's a little extortion among
friends?"

—*Bill Watterson*

Picture this: you have a health problem. A chronic one, that requires a regular supply of prescription treatments, whether they be medications, physical therapy, medical supplies, or what-have-you. You've had a lot going on in your life lately and you know you haven't been keeping up on things like you should have been. Maybe it's *because* of this health problem that you haven't, because you're in pain, or your mental health is in the tank. In any case, your rent is past due, the car's check engine light is on, you're child's school is calling – *again...*

You call your doctor because you need a renewal of your order, and *they* tell you they won't do it unless you get an appointment first, or labs, or fill out some papers.

Is this right? Is it justifiable? To be held hostage like this? Well... it depends on the exact circumstance. Let's take a step back, and have a look:

Suppose you haven't seen your doctor in five years. A lot can happen in that time. When you finally do go in, they're basically starting from scratch. Anything over a year old is probably worth rechecking (labs, imaging, and so forth). So, in that case, yeah, you need that appointment. A lot of what we do is very individual-dependent and the one constant about life, is *change*. So cut your doc a break and get in there, even though it means taking time off work, getting a babysitter, scrounging in the couch cushions for the copay, and calling an Uber.

What about if there's something new in your life? You've developed a health problem you've not experienced before? I've told folks many times that *nothing beats eyes on the target* (this is why I regarded telehealth during the pandemic as a necessary evil). Again, set yourself and your provider up for success and get in there so they can see firsthand what's up. We're not just reading your vitals and looking over your labs. We're watching how you sit, walk, talk, and breathe. We're examining your skin and how you answer questions. There is a lot that goes on from the second we walk in the room that's relevant, that you just can't get on a video call. (And I've been known to ask my front desk staff how the patient looked in the waiting room!) They may even see something unexpected while they're looking other things over that can really add insight to the situation. I've had that happen many times.

But what if it's a stable problem? Just a refill on your Zoloft? Again, it depends. A lot of meds, especially those used in mental health, can really trash your immune system and the right thing to do is monitor labs or vital signs, sometimes quite frequently. To not do so would put *you* at risk for some serious complications that are worse than what you're dealing with now. Other very common meds are hard on your kidneys, or your liver. For the same reasons, these systems need to be monitored regularly.

On the other hand, I've seen doctors take this attitude to extremes. When I was a resident doing my obstetrics rotations it seemed very common for OB-GYN's to refuse to refill birth control prescriptions for healthy women unless she came in for her annual pap. This made no sense to me. Sure, we want to do screenings to prevent disease, but if the consequence of withholding meds is a possible pregnancy with all the risks that entails, is it worth it? As it was, a few years later new pap recommendations were published that greatly reduced the number of screenings and made a lot of those (let's call them what they were) bullyings unnecessary. (However, Depo shots are different and fall into that high-risk med category. Getting a shot while unknowingly pregnant can lead to some *serious* consequences).

Likewise for depression meds. Was it right to threaten stopping treatment for the sake of a checkup? Even fairly benign drugs like the SSRIs (Zoloft, Paxil, and so forth) can be nasty if high doses are stopped suddenly. And often folks are put on these meds due to suicidal thoughts. Again, is the risk of the untreated condition worth extorting a visit out of the patient?

And then one gets into the moral issue of denying care altogether. A trend I saw all too often (among pediatricians especially) was to refuse care to children whose parents declined vaccinations. There's been plenty of talk in our society about (and by) anti-vaxxers, but I've done a lot of work in the Amish community and they have historically avoided immunizations. For them it's more on religious grounds (or more faith in their own healing) rather than what some celebrity said on social media. Do they not deserve to get their strep throats treated just because they didn't get their MMR? It made me feel those docs were more worried about their malpractice premiums or their corporate overlords than actually caring for sick folks. I had my shots, and so did my kids. I wasn't worried that I was going to bring something home. And I always tried to keep the appointments moving so no one was hanging out in the waiting room for too long. I understand the epidemiological risks, the concept of herd immunity, and all of it, but at the end of the day we as doctors are treating an *individual* sitting in front of us, a living person with hopes, dreams, fears, and responsibilities. We are in a position to help them and, according to society, are obligated by that position to do so. And a core principle of medical care is still that the patient has autonomy. They can choose for themselves. It's the whole reason we have this thing called 'informed consent'. Is it truly morally right to tell a suffering human being that you could help, but you flat-out won't, because of some administrative rule? Or worse, because your personal opinions are at odds with their health choices?

Another aspect of this hostage-taking is when political goals get in the way of health care. Here in Ohio there's an imminent collision right now between the dexter-side of the political spectrum and the transgender community over whether or not transition-specific care is even going to be allowed. The political side of the issue wants to make such things unavailable unless the patient is being managed by an endocrinologist, a psychiatrist, *and* a medical ethicist. Now it may not be a bad idea to suggest these experts be consulted, but I get wary of requiring anything as a blanket condition. If we're going to just legislate how everything is to be done, why have licenses and medical boards at all? After all, any fool can follow a script.

I consider my role with my patients as a consultant, or a facilitator. They have the problem, I have the insight to suggest a solution. I know what will help them, and how it will coexist with everything else they have going on. But it's their body, and their life. They get to choose. They're the ones that will be living with the consequences of whatever we as a team decide to do – good or bad. It's my responsibility to explain everything to them in a way they can understand. I'm the one who needs to show why my solution is the best – or conversely, listen to the patient's opinion because they may have another (maybe even better!) idea (it's another core principle that we *learn from our patients*). Because I can tell you, if your patient doesn't want to follow your advice, they probably won't so you'd better work something out with them and make them a partner in the decision making.

People are people, and we are all different. And as long as we're being honest with our doctors, no policy maker in a marbled hall, think tank, or national association will know better than they, what we need.

And as physicians, if we're not treating our patients as individuals we aren't really doctors at all. We're only puppets in lab coats.

SJA '24

'Woke' Med School?!?

"Remember that you will never reach a higher standard than you yourself set. Then set your mark high, and step by step, even though it be by painful effort, by self-denial and sacrifice, ascend the whole length of the ladder of progress."

—*Ellen Gould White*

Okay, let me start right off by stating for the record that I don't have a lot of experience with discrimination (Gasp! Shock and awe!) I'm a white guy, after all. As white as they come: ancestors on one side from Wales and Austria, on the other from Finland. There's no hidden Native Americans or other people of color in my line, and I've gone *way* back in that search.

But I do have family members who've had to contend daily with DWB, so I can say with certainty that racism (at least) is alive and well here. Frankly I'm amazed. I've been around a good while (I grew up watching the original *Star Trek* on reruns, if that tells you anything) and I've been hearing about how we need to stop discrimination for over fifty years. And yet time and again I'm just dumbfounded when some public figure that stumps loudly in the public square for Diversity/Equity/Inclusion, aka DEI, will get caught making some incredibly offensive remarks when they don't realize the mic is still hot.

And then I think, when are we going to learn this lesson? Why is this still a problem?

Because old habits are hard to break, I guess, and some people will always blame their troubles on someone else and carry that grudge like it's got a handle. I recently saw a documentary on Nazi Germany in which it was revealed a US Army psychiatrist by the name of Dr. Douglas M. Kelley examined high-ranking Nazis after the war (including Hermann Göring himself). He specifically wanted to determine what mental illness made them the way they were, and was very surprised to find that, as a rule, they suffered from no consistent disorder. As far as mental balance was concerned, they were just an ordinary cross-section of humanity, which meant that what they did could potentially be done by *anyone* (if you doubt that, look up the *Rheinwiesenlager*). It was a realization that later weighed heavily on Dr. Kelley.

It's because of this ongoing problem with people being all too willing to judge for very superficial reasons that we have DEI policies in the first place. Why they are institutionalized is really no surprise to me: one of the defining ideas of the founding of this country was that 'all men are created equal'. Put aside any post-modern criticisms here: I was taught from early grade school this did in fact mean *everyone in mankind*. We (meaning the US citizenry of the late 1700's) weren't trying to deliberately exclude women, blacks, Irish, Chinese, or what-have-you. I understood in no uncertain terms that it meant that everyone had a right to the pursuit of happiness. (That was the stated ideal. Obviously a very great many have not lived up to that.) But it's important to note that we were *not* guaranteed *achieving* that happiness. That was up to us.

The idea is that everyone here should have an equal place *at the starting line*. But once that gun goes off and we start sprinting, how far we get will be up to us. Up to our wit, our endurance, and our cleverness.

So how does this fit into the developing debate over DEI policies in medical education? Let's go back in the process to the beginning:

There's no doubt that socioeconomic standing plays a *huge* role in one's success in school, and how well prepared one is for real life afterwards. Too many studies have proven this, and how impoverished neighborhoods lead to impoverished citizens. DEI has a real place here – this is where we get everyone on the same starting line, and this is how we do it. It is vitally important at the primary and secondary education levels because for the vast majority of us, where we go to school depends solely on where we live. We don't get to choose. The bus shows up, and off we go.

But in college it's a different story. You don't have to go to the local community college, you can choose another school. Granted it may be another community college in the town where your aunt lives, but you at least have *some* choice. Maybe you have a skill in sports or academics that can secure you some funding which will broaden those choices. Maybe there's a scholarship you can qualify for. I went to med school at Case Western, but I had to sell my soul to the Navy to do it, augmented by a significant scholarship I received from the Joseph Collins Foundation for my avocation as an artist. The analogy is that this is where your abilities, your drive, your determination and your resourcefulness will determine how far down the track you get, and how fast. You don't have to start off at Harvard. I got into Case after starting my first two years at Kent State's Geauga campus – literally the local community college. And then I worked my butt off. And it wasn't a straight shot afterwards, either. It took me ten years to finish eight years of schooling, and that was *with* a full semester of college credit for my time in the Army.

The problem I see in implementing DEI criteria, in medical school admissions and evaluations in particular, is that we aren't just talking some general degree here that is useful for little more than getting you into an HR office (let's face it, for most corporate jobs, that's just what that BS or BA is for). It's a very technical field with exacting performance requirements. As an Army vet it feels a lot like the debate over allowing women into combat roles. Women want to fight, I thought? Let them! But they'll have to meet the same physical requirements as the men. They'll have to be able to sprint with that 40-pound ruck a hundred meters just as fast as the rest of us when the artillery starts dropping, because you can't slow down for someone who's just not up to the task without putting your whole mission in jeopardy. You want to get paid for the job? You have to do the job. The way it needs to be done. Not scaled back to suit your abilities (or lack of same).

There's nothing wrong with encouraging people to shoot for the moon. There's nothing wrong with getting them a place on the starting line with everyone else. If someone has what it takes they should have the chance to make use of it. But once that gun goes off, they either perform, or they don't. And a doc that doesn't perform, is a detriment to their patients. No one deserves that.

*This page is blank because I added a picture in the
next section and couldn't fix the formatting*

SJA '24

Babies And Bathwater

"Society's revenge matched its fright."
—Barbara W. Tuchman

Opium has a long history of use for medicinal purposes. As far back as the Neolithic age it was being used for anesthesia, general pain relief, and as a sleep aid. It was mentioned in the Ebers Papyrus, one of the oldest medical texts of Ancient Egypt, and the works of Galen and Dioscorides.

Its use for recreational purposes came along somewhat later. Some of the earliest reports mention it in the possession of soldiers returning from the Crusades. By the 14th Century recreational use was well established in the Near East. By the late 15th Century it was in China, and in Western Europe in the 18th.

Of course, along with opium's burgeoning use as a recreational substance, addictions developed with all the accompanying negative effects. This alarmed the Chinese Daoguang Emperor and in 1834 he tried to end the smuggling of opium into China from Turkish sources through British and American 'intermediaries' (like FDR's grandpa Warren Delano, Jr. – look him up if you get a chance). This culminated in a standoff in 1839 in which the Chinese seized and destroyed 1,300 metric tons of opium and eventually led to the bombardment of Dinghai by the Royal Navy on behalf of their less-than-legal-minded private entrepreneurs. China lost the First Opium War and was

forced to cede Hong Kong to Britain and pay a fine of twenty-one million dollars to replace the lost opium stocks. I don't think even the Escobars of our time ever thought of demanding an entire city as payback.

In 1853 there was another attempt by China to stop the opium trade and again, they were walloped by the British (with French help this time) who actually occupied the famed Forbidden City. More reparations were paid and the opium trade was legalized, foreign 'traders' (as they were now legitimized) were granted travel rights in China and everyone in Merry Ol' England breathed easier knowing they could get their laudanum.

The rise of opiates as a recreational drug in the United States in more modern times is pretty well known and I'm not going to belabor it here. Nor do I intend to minimize the horrendous human cost of opiate addictions and overdoses. I've known people that suffered from these as well as other addictions and I've seen the cost up close and firsthand. I've seen what it does to those left behind as well. But like any high-profile crisis, there's a lot of posturing among our leadership to make a show of how the 'good fight' is being fought, while the fallout of tactics used is being swept under the rug.

Now don't get me wrong. Opiates used to be handed out *way* too cavalierly. In the mid 2000's I did my residency at MetroHealth Medical Center in Cleveland. We had a really impressive ER: 72 beds, Level 1 Trauma capable, the whole bit. But what I kept seeing were folks who would arrive in the ER with some acute injury, like a back strain, a rotator cuff injury, or the like, and would be given a couple weeks' worth of Percocet and told to follow up in the Family Practice clinic – pretty standard fare across the country, at the time. But we were busy, too, and it would take three or four weeks for them to get an appointment on the other side of the foyer. The patients would stretch their meds and by the time I got to see them they were already developing dependency.

Not long afterwards the powers-that-be started putting restrictions on this freewheeling prescribing by the ER's. At least at this point they seemed to recognize this was a real part of the problem. Then In 2016 the CDC released new guidelines in managing *chronic* pain [1,] and things took a turn.

Chronic pain is much different from what you get with a broken bone or a bad tooth. Just ask anyone with diabetic neuropathy, degenerative disc disease, ulcerative colitis, or any one of a number of cancers. It can be *unre-lenting*. And it won't get better. You're not going to heal to the point the pain will go away. And that pain can put you in bed, unable to move, though sometimes even that doesn't give you relief. It can make you sick, angry, and desperate. One large study in Sweden of over seventeen thousand patients found a *51% increase* in suicidality in chronic pain sufferers [2.]

What the CDC were trying to do was to put some kind of standardization and cohesiveness on approaches to managing chronic pain. Honestly their guidelines were pretty good. The general idea was that meds were being too easily dispensed and thus too available on the street, and the CDC recommended that every pain regimen have a clear reason for its existence (meaning a proven diagnosis), and a well-defined treatment goal. In the case of the chronic pain patient, often this goal could only be to control the pain so they could work, take care of their family, and otherwise be a content and contributing member of society. Sometimes it's just not possible to expect that they could become pain-free and not need any treatment. The guidelines also advised reevaluating the regimen at certain points to make sure you as the provider were considering other options for pain control, and provided education on signs to watch for in your clinic visits for inappropriate use.

It was the *implementation* of these suggestions on the front lines, by state medical boards, pharmacy boards, insurers, and hospital systems, that caused the problems. The regulatory boards saw an opportunity to show the public they were actively involved in combating the opiate epidemic. Recommendations were made into hard-and-fast rules. Suggestions for treatment checkpoints became inviolate limits. Tapering off meds was the plan for *everyone* except, generously, the terminally ill. Sauron-like scrutiny was turned on anyone poking their head above the berm, no matter the reason and in spite of the claim that people would be 'grandfathered' in to the new treatment goals.

Ever fearful of losing government funding, or worse, hard-won licenses, hospital systems and pharmacies simply started to severely curtail opiate prescribing rather than really take a look at individual patients and make certain, as the CDC had suggested, that what they were getting was indicated and effective. Despite what could legitimately be described as patient abandonment, many organizations simply stopped prescribing controlled meds altogether.

And the med boards went right along with this by targeting anyone that wasn't jumping in the boat with them.

The rebound of this was immediate. People still had their pain. And, like it or not, many had become dependent and faced withdrawal. So where did they go? To the street. Where they were self-medicating, without a trained provider to monitor doses, frequencies, side effects and interactions. Where no pharmacist could guarantee a certified supply chain. Where no manufacturer was making sure the oxycodone wasn't being supplanted with something more potent (read that: smaller doses required and thus cheaper) like fentanyl. And overdoses soared.

In Ohio the new rules went into effect at the very end of 2018. By this time opiate overdose deaths were peaking and looked like they were starting to drop. But at the same time the new rules were being put into effect they jumped up again and continued to rise a total of *46%* through 2021[3,] a trend mirrored in nationwide data [4.] Here we've seen a slight reduction in 2022, and I'm anxious to see if 2023 proves this is a trend or just a statistical variation.

The CDC recognized what was happening and issued a paper in 2019 warning against the inappropriate application of their guidelines [5], but it remains to be seen if the regulatory boards are going to be as quick to get off the bandwagon as they were to get on it.

There's no doubt the opiate problem needs to be cleaned up. Opiates are *dangerous* medications if improperly used. But they can be lifesaving when they're done right. And doing them right requires treating individual people, each of whom has their own story, on a one-on-one basis and not just trying to make 'one-size-fits-most' dictates from an ivory-colored concrete tower.

*If I had more to say in the last section this page
wouldn't be blank*

Damned If We Do, Damned If We Don't?

"It's easy to make a mess when you're not the one who has to clean it up."

—*Criss Jami*

No one will argue that we are having an epidemic of opiate overdose deaths. Nor is there any doubt that the medical community had a big role in getting this whole thing started [1].

But my question for *you* is, what do you think, *now that we're here*? Let's put aside the finger-pointing of whose fault it is. That ship sailed a long time ago and we're abandoned on the dock with the city burning behind us. How should we be handling the mess that's been left behind?

Our state leaders made sure we knew they had set up task forces, consulted experts and enacted policies. Major hospital systems were also quick to get in line. Narcan became widely available, as was patient education, both of which I strongly agree with. The problem that I saw was *overreactions*. Like toddlers caught with their hands in the cookie jar state leaders and hospital CEOs started blubbering apologies and promises to '*never do it again*'.

In Ohio this really seemed to take hold after the CDC issued their 'Guideline for Prescribing Opioids for Chronic Pain' in 2016 [2], a good policy that recommended benchmarks for assessing treatment and sound suggestions for monitoring. But the State Medical Board of Ohio went one better and issued a new rule (supposedly) based on these guidelines but <u>implemented</u> with an iron fist. I've heard too many stories, from patients, friends, and family members about the fear of the SMBO driving providers to just completely stop writing controlled meds altogether – despite the fact that this is tantamount to abandonment and dramatically adding to the problem [3,4]. These providers and their employers excuse themselves by offering referrals to Pain Management – never mind the Pain Management providers are now swamped and are booking 6-8 months out; are themselves backtracking many of their treatments; or that there is little incentive for new doctors to get into the field to replace the ones getting out.

Now add the DEA forcing supply reductions [5,6]. 13% down in two years is a chronic pain patient going without their meds for a *half a week every month*. People use these meds to function, so what now? Cutting work hurts the economy. Cutting out family life creates more problems than I can begin to address. Is this what we really want [7]? The DEA has petulantly wailed '*it wasn't me!*' [8] but others disagree and aren't afraid to call them out in federal court [9].

Pain Management's goal is to help people function, and it takes a lot of different approaches to work: psychology, physical therapy, multiple types of meds, alternative medicine... all have their role to play. But removing an entire class of meds and terrorizing prescribers so they are afraid to do the job they've trained *years* for is not an answer. The DEA is made up of law enforcement officers, not doctors. They've been known to 'reach out' to the medical community here and there [10], but *I* haven't found any record of any doctors actually *on staff*.

Like it or not, right now many people *are* addicted, whoever's fault it is. Leaving them writhing in pain, sweating through withdrawal, or desperately buying unregulated or fake Percocets probably laced with fentanyl, just so we can look like the good guys, flies in the face of our ideals and is morally *criminal.*

To its credit the CDC recognized the posturing by these lesser groups and tried to put a stop to it [11,12,13]. It's anyone's guess, though, how long it will take for a little compassion to seep back into the pain management world. Being able to tell the public you're doing something – *anything* – is an addiction all its own.

This page is blank so you can collect your thoughts before plunging ahead

Why I No Longer Practice Medicine
In Ohio

"Fairness is not an attitude. It's a profes-
sional skill that must be developed and
exercised."

—*Brit Hume*

I grew up on my grandparents' farm in rural Ohio. After
high school I worked in polymer factories for fifteen
years because I wasn't sure what I wanted to be when I
grew up (!) but eventually I decided med school was the
way to go (!!), and at the age of 32 I joined the Ohio Army
National Guard for the GI Bill, and started college.

I spent six years in the Guard as a cavalry scout and
loved it. I reached the rank of sergeant and graduated Kent
State with my BS in Mathematics in 2001.

I was accepted into med school and started at Case Western Reserve School of Medicine on my thirty-eighth birthday. I switched branches to the Navy and they gave me a scholarship to pay my tuition, which was supplemented by a sizable grant from the Joseph Collins Foundation. Now I was a naval officer on Inactive Reserve. Med school was challenging, more so because I had a family in tow, but I made it through, got my MD in 2007 and started residency in Family Medicine. I had had a vision for myself from the beginning of this odyssey of being the 'country doctor'.

After residency I shipped off to active duty with the Navy to the Marine Corps Air-Ground Combat Center in 29 Palms, and when that was done came back home and started working for a local hospital. We set up a clinic in the same town from which I had graduated high school, and for several years things were going well.

Then the pandemic hit and the clinic closed down. I struck out on my own as an independent doc at a small private clinic.

On June 9, 2021, the DEA raided the clinic and accused me of illegally prescribing opiates. Three years before, the State Medical Board of Ohio had asked me about my prescribing practices; I had answered their questions, provided them with records, and thought the issue was settled since nothing more was said. But the Fed heard about it, and ran with it.

I hired a lawyer and voluntarily gave up my DEA certificate. At first I thought I had a good shot of defending myself. After all, they were saying that I had been handing out oxycodone without appropriate diagnoses and without regard for my patients' health. At the time I had 1,127 patients in my care, of which all of 73 were on chronic pain management for things like Crohn's Disease, Complex Regional Pain Syndrome, or Spinal Stenosis. I knew I had always been very particular about my documentation, and always had definite reasons for treatment and clear goals for my people in mind, just like the CDC advised. These folks were *functioning*. They were holding down jobs, caring for their families, and had a decent quality of life. They had been seen by Physical Therapy, Aquatherapy, Orthopedics, Neurology, Neurosurgery, Psychology, Pain Management and Rheumatology. They were involved in acupuncture and were managed, not only on opiates, but neuropathics, NSAIDs and topical treatments. And I was not just 'dabbling' in pain management: I had done multiple rotations at the pain clinic at the Wade Park VA under the direct tutelage of one of the area's top pain docs, and had also been taught one-on-one in end-of-life care for hospice patients (which often requires the concurrent use of opiates and benzodiazepines) by one of Ohio's top geriatricians (who, by the way, offered me a job in 2022, though I had to turn him down because I didn't want to try to get my DEA certificate back).

But by November 2021 it was clear to my attorney that things were not going to go well. His take was, I could take it to trial, but it would cost over a hundred thousand dollars and there was a very good chance I would still lose and go to prison for twenty years (you know what they say... you can't fight city hall – and I was a lone, independent doctor against the Fed). I had been through a divorce in the past and knew from painful experience that court is *nothing* like it is on TV. It's not a chess game where evidence and testimony jockey for position and the perp is backed into a corner from which he can't escape, or the unjustly accused are exonerated when the truth is revealed.

It's intimidation, inflammatory language, and whether the court even feels like admitting the evidence you have.

The other option was to take a plea for health care fraud, to say that I had brought people in for unnecessary visits. Still a felony, still untrue, but much less likely to carry a prison sentence and no need for that six-figure court battle.

What was I to do? I had a wife and ten-year-old son at home. I would have had to sell the house and pretty much everything else to go to trial and then they would have been homeless at the very least, whether I won or lost. And a public defender? In Ohio PD's are only free if you're destitute. If you have assets (like that house), you're expected to liquidate them to contribute to the legal fees. I was literally stuck in the gap – no ready cash to just pay for my defense outright, yet not broke enough to qualify for any real help.

So, I took the plea. Twelve counts, for twelve visits. Out of seventy-odd folks over seven years. My conviction was formally entered on June 15, 2023, and I started 6 months of house arrest.

What amazed me about that part of the legal process is how little our judicial branch knows about the medical field. I was ostracized in the pre-sentencing report for 'often prescribing well in excess of the CDC-recommended maximum of 90 morphine equivalents per day (90 MED)'. For a little context, in 2016 the CDC issued recommendations on opiate prescribing. That 90 MED dose was in fact a benchmark. It was *not a hard limit*. It was a point at which you were to 'press pause' and make sure you were doing the right things for the right reasons [1]. (Fun fact: when you take a plea you get to write out your own confession! It's called the 'Acceptance of Responsibility Statement' and it's where you get to write in your own words how and why you did what it's claimed you did. Because if you don't, and you insist on protesting your innocence, you'll get branded as unrepentant. And believe me, you don't want that to happen.)

In the meantime, the Medical Board remembered me and took action against my license. I wasn't terribly concerned at first. I had read their expert report and the allegations they made, and I had rebuttals for every point. It was stunning, really, their expert report itself: wrong dates of service, claims things weren't done, which were clearly documented in the record, or conversely claims of statements made, that weren't... at times I wondered if their expert had even read my patients' charts, or had simply ctrl-F'd through the whole thing.

It should be noted at this point that the State Medical Board of Ohio had, on December 23, 2018, codified the CDC's 2016 guidelines (supposedly with a grandfather clause for people already on doses of pain meds in excess of that 90 MED mark, which would have covered the handful of patients in my case). It is also important to note that on April 24, 2019, the CDC itself released a paper warning against an overly-zealous application of what were only supposed to be guidelines, as 'rules'[2]. They were beginning to see that med boards, hospital systems, and insurers across the country were interpreting their advice too rigidly and inappropriately cutting off patients' meds, and in fact were quite possibly causing an *increase* in opiate deaths[3]. I'm not going to speculate here as to why that was; other folks have already done that[4].

The hearing for my prescribing practices was set for late January 2024. Once the felony conviction took hold, though, the Med Board decided they now had a separate issue and held a hearing on September 25, 2023, for the conviction. At that hearing (done by videoconference) I tried to explain what I felt had happened, thinking that a group tasked with setting policy would be interested in knowing these things, but the prosecutor instead felt I was making excuses and showing no remorse. The Board then set a date for December 13, 2023, to make a formal decision.

Now let me paint you a picture: the State Medical Board of Ohio holds their meetings in what used to be the Ohio State Supreme Court courtroom, and they had specifically decided against any redecorating when they took over the space. There is an imposing raised dais seating the twelve board members, and twenty-foot ceilings. This makes you, standing alone on the floor before them, feel very small. My attorney and I had five minutes (conveniently counted down by a timer!) to make our final statements. We reminded them there were two cases before them, and the original case, for which we had my rebuttals, our own expert witnesses, and patient testimonies prepared, was due for hearing in six weeks. We asked simply that they take no action on my license that day but wait until January so we could present our defense.

The Board then deliberated. For all of five more minutes. One Board member asked the others if it would be such a bad thing to wait until the next hearing to see what we had, but that notion was quickly squashed. I had pled guilty to the health care fraud charge, it was argued, and that was enough. They 'didn't need to hear any more' and I 'did not deserve to be a physician in the State of Ohio'.

Again I was amazed at the cavalier attitude and apparent lack of real-world experience present. For example, I was criticized for expressing a lack of faith in pill counts as they could be easily faked. These meds are all stamped with codes, I was told, making it easy to see if the count has been 'supplemented'.

Now let me take a moment to talk about pharmacies. They're businesses, after all, and will buy their stock wherever they can get a good price. Oxycodone itself is available in the US from Veranova, Noramco, Chattem Chem, Siegfried USA, Mallinckroot Chem, and Penick Corp, and the 30mg dose alone comes in no less than eight different code/color/size combinations (per the Epocrates Drug Database):

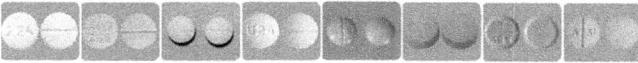

Sometimes pharmacies will get their meds from one supplier, sometimes from another. Sometimes they won't be able to give a patient a full script and will issue a partial fill and make up the balance when the next shipment comes in – from wherever. Sometimes patients will get their meds filled a few days early, because of a holiday weekend for example, and again, might be given a different looking pill that gets mixed in with the tail end of last months' script. And don't forget the folks on PRN meds, who may end up with a bottle in the car, one in their purse, and one at work, all getting filled at different rates. The point here is that, even a *completely legitimate* patient who is *absolutely lockstep* in taking their meds may end up with a mix of pills through no fault of their own. Was I then supposed to fail that patient's pill count and cut them off, with all the potential dire consequences of such a course [5]?

I also had only a certain amount of faith in urine drug screens. I did them, but I knew there is an entire industry out there to beat them. After all, it's possible to pick up a kit at a store *on your way to your doctor's office* for that surprise call-in that will fix your urine for you.

My solution was to see them. Often. To lay eyes on them, see how they acted, how they were dressed and groomed, how they answered questions, whether they made eye contact, who brought them, and how was *that* person acting in the waiting room? How were their vitals, and their physical exam? Were there inconsistencies in their histories? How were they doing? How was their pain? Was it controlled? What could we do to make it better, now, and long-term?

Was it a perfect method? Of course not. But I felt if someone was gaming the system it would be a lot harder to keep up appearances month after month than it would be to pick up a handful of pills off the street to refill a bottle. But *this* strategy, apparently, was tantamount to bringing patients in 'unnecessarily' and constituted 'health care fraud'.

In any case, after just a few minutes a vote was held and my Ohio license was gone. I had had no chance to present my defense. I could appeal, sure, and spend another fifty thousand, but I had seen what I was dealing with and was not impressed that anyone was willing to listen.

The real kick in the teeth is that, not eight months after the DEA filed charges against me, the U.S. Supreme Court ruled in *Ruan v. United States* that the conviction of illegal prescribing required proving the physician acted 'knowingly or intentionally' in defiance of his patients' best interests [6]. That stance alone would have greatly improved the odds in my favor and might have justified taking the case to trial. A victory there would have eliminated the felony charge and all the negative stigma that followed. *Ruan v. United States* is a valuable ruling for those dealing with this now, and I'm glad to see it codified... it was just too late for me, and sometimes that's just how it goes.

My real issue was with the Medical Board. I got through the criminal case, and the house arrest. But when I went in to defend my license things were much different. Did I have a good defense against the Medical Board's concerns of misconduct? I thought I had. Had I followed the guidelines set by my peers, that were in effect at the time in question? I thought so. Had the State done an even *barely* adequate job reviewing my records? In my opinion, certainly not. Was I granted my constitutional right to due process? My lawyer felt I hadn't been.

But now we will never know. The Board had 'heard enough'.

And that, ladies and gentlemen, is why I no longer practice medicine in the State of Ohio.

Part Three:

Coping

With health, with life, with the fallout of
bad decisions...

Living With Dementia

"One person caring about another repre-
sents life's greatest value."

—*Jim Rohn*

Miilia Maria Kotiilia Kananen was my grandmother on my dad's side. She was born in 1913 to Johannes and Briita Kananen, immigrants who left Finland in 1908 when it was still part of the Russian Empire. She grew up in Williamsfield, OH (on the Pennsylvania state line), and in 1936 she married my grandfather, Vaughn Arnold. They had a farm a little further west, in Huntsburg, and raised corn, cattle, and then chickens.

She spent her life as a tough farm woman. She loved plants and had a greenhouse attached to the house. She would find toads in the yard and bring them into the greenhouse, and would frequently pick them up and talk to them – and they would chirp back to her!

She was 92 when my grandfather passed in 2005. It became clear pretty quickly that she had had dementia for some time, and that he had been covering for her. We found she would leave windows open around the house, and then become angry because someone was leaving windows open around the house! Laundry would pile up in the corners (keep in mind she had always been very particular about keeping a clean house) and blamed it on women that floated in the air and dropped it through doors in the ceiling.

We had her in a nursing home for a while but this became too expensive and we brought her home to live with us. Everything was going about as well as could be expected for a time, but it is a characteristic of Alzheimer's Type Dementia that the victim regresses, thinking themselves younger and younger, and there came a day when Grandma was once again a rebellious sixteen-year old and we couldn't manage her any longer.

She eventually passed, in 2008, and while she was needing a lot of care at the time, was not as far gone as some people I've had the privilege of looking after. I've done a lot of work in nursing homes, and I've had a fair number of my patients progress to the point that they even forget how to eat. You could give them a fork and they would look at it, mystified, before picking up their food with their fingers.

Dementia is a heartbreak. The longer it goes on the worse the heartbreak gets. People become as little children, and need all the care and safeguarding that a toddler does.

This is our responsibility, as those who are still possessed of our faculties. It is a responsibility we owe to those who made sacrifices on our behalf, both individually and as a society, and one I have always taken very seriously.

This page is blank because <u>I</u> had to collect <u>my</u> thoughts before plunging ahead

113

The Good Samaritan—Which One Are We?

"Everyone wants to be the Sun, to lighten up someone's life, but why not be the moon, to brighten in the darkest hour?"

—*Conscious Magazine,*
author unknown

I'm guessing most folks out there have heard the story of the Good Samaritan found in the New Testament. In case you haven't, or you don't really recall all the details sufficiently for it to be useful as one of life's metaphors, here's a quick refresher:

In Biblical times Judea and Samaria shared a border. The people of these nations also shared an intense hatred for each other, for reasons I won't get into here. Suffice it to say each felt their neighbors were about two steps below scum of the earth.

In this context Jesus tells the following story to a lawyer who wants to know the definition of a 'neighbor': One day a traveler was making his way along the road from Jerusalem to Jericho. His nationality is not explicitly stated but it's pretty clear from the context he's a Jew. The road to Jericho had been notorious as being the 'Way of Blood' due to all the robberies that took place there, and this poor soul became the next statistic. He was attacked by thieves, robbed, beaten, and left for dead on the side of the road.

In time a priest happens along the road, sees the man laying there, and passes by on the other side. Then follows a Levite – not a priest, but still a member of the Israelite tribe that was especially tasked with providing men for the priesthood – who also passes by on the other side. It isn't until a Samaritan (of all people!) happens along and feels compassion for the man's plight that the victim finally is picked up, cleaned off, and taken to an inn to recover at the Samaritan's expense.

The obvious lesson here is that the two passersby that one would expect should be inspired to help, did not. It was the guy that probably had a lot of reasons not to, that did. Now to be fair to the priest and the Levite, we shouldn't assume that they saw the man and actually went out of their way to avoid him. Maybe they were already on the other side of the road and just kept going. Perhaps they didn't realize he was still alive and just assumed he was another unfortunate victim (then again, they didn't check). Maybe they were on more important missions that meant they couldn't spare the time. All these factors have been debated by scholars, though I feel that's missing the point: this story was a parable, not a history. This wasn't an actual anecdote about four real people. It was a tale made to illustrate a point, and so I feel we should just stick to the obvious lesson.

All that aside, the reason so many people are at least passingly familiar with the story is that it is often used as an example of charity without prejudice. And I think it's common for those folks that like to use this tend to identify with the Samaritan. We all like to be the good guys, right?

I'm a sucker for fun adventure movies, and one that I really like from about ten years ago was 'Jack The Giant Slayer' starring Nicholas Hoult and Stanley Tucci. It has a lot of funny parts, and a few very profound ones as well, and one line in particular struck me in a way that I don't usually feel in movies like this. Tucci's character Roderick, (the Bad Guy) is about to finish off Elmont (played by Ewan McGregor), the captain of the king's guard. He observes, "YOU think you're the hero of this story. *Don't you know, we ALL think that?*"

And that is very, very true. It's not a bad thing, really, that we see ourselves as the hero. It can inspire us to better behavior. On the downside, though, we can often lull ourselves into a false sense of superiority in seeing ourselves as the Samaritan when in practice we are more like the Levite: always too busy to stop, or convincing ourselves that the poor soul on the side of the road is beyond any help we could give, without really having a look to be sure. Or even worse, to feel the other guy has done something to deserve this misfortune, and who are we to question the judgement of God, Karma, or the Fates?

The irony of this point of view is that nearly all moral systems, whether they are based on formal religion, individualized spirituality, or altruistic secularism, promote the practice of charity without *any* conditions. There is no allowance made nor exception granted for how busy we are, or how important we may feel our tasks may be, or especially for passing judgement on the recipient's worthiness.

This makes sense since quite often it's hard for us to appreciate the struggles another has experienced. How can we rank the moral superiority of our duties versus another's immediate need? How can we assess the justifiability of the events that left this victim bereft? Moral systems as a rule lay the real benefit of showing compassion and charity towards another in the lap of the giver – more so if this involves some sacrifice on our part, and even if the other guy *did* bring his fate down upon himself.

I think it's a useful exercise for all of us to take some time every so often to dust off this old saw and have a look at how we fit into it, *especially* when we see that metaphorical heap on the side of the road and we're debating if we should stop or not.

SJA'24

A Necessary Inhumanity

Detachment is not indifference. It is the
prerequisite for effective involvement....
It is only when we want nothing for
ourselves that we are able to see clearly
into others' needs and understand how
to serve them.

—*Mahatma Gandhi*

First, do no harm. It's a litany that is heard quite often in malpractice circles. The common conception is that this is a premier part of the Hippocratic Oath that aspiring physicians are supposed to take at the beginning of their careers.

But there are some aspects of this common wisdom that aren't quite accurate. First of all is the notion that every med student takes the Oath. Truth is, many med schools no longer give it to their incoming classes, a fact I was quite surprised to find out when I was at Case taking *my* oath, and the point was made that they were becoming the exception.

Next is the Hippocratic Oath itself. As its name suggests, it originates in the writings of Hippocrates, the famous physician of Classical Greek antiquity, and sets a framework for medical ethics. The meat of his oath actually was to respect one's teachers and the knowledge that had been gained by our predecessors; to keep things told in confidence, secret; and to abstain from deliberately causing death. It does contain statements against causing harm, though these are not given any kind of primacy over anything else. We are not specifically told that our *first* priority should be to not do harm. That, in effect, would suggest it is somehow better to do nothing, than to do something and risk it being the wrong thing.

On the contrary, medicine is *all about* managing the risks. *Anything* a doctor can do can go wrong – *even doing nothing*. Make no mistake, sometimes it's valuable to know when to keep your hands off a problem until it develops further, or just goes away (we call that 'treating with a tincture of time'). But we didn't get into this line of work so we could stand by until we had an absolute guarantee of diagnosis and plan. There is only *one* guarantee in this field. Putting a rule in place of doing no harm above any other course action is futile and counterproductive.

This makes sense, actually. There are plenty of times one must inflict damage in order to address a health problem. If you've ever had to remove a splinter from a child's finger you know what I'm talking about. And there's a reason we refer to incisions as 'surgical wounds'. And consider the sometimes brutal side effects of chemotherapy, which can be so bad people will literally choose death. (Sometimes it's just better to end with three good months, rather than twelve bad ones.) And quite often it just isn't possible to treat one health problem without making another one worse.

This is one thing that sets physicians apart from any other health care folks: the development of what's been described as a 'necessary inhumanity'. It's also been called 'clinical detachment', but I prefer the former term; it seems better suited to showing there needs to be a face-to-face relationship between the doctor and the patient. We're in it, and we know it hurts, but we also know how important it is. And yes, we *are* going to look at ourselves in the mirror later, and ponder...

A better interpretation of the original Greek of the Oath would probably be 'to alleviate suffering'. This recognizes that sometimes we *must* harm in the process of healing. Alleviating suffering without engaging in futile efforts to improve health is the basis of palliative care as well as mass-casualty triage. It recognizes that sometimes there just isn't anything to be done to make things better that isn't going to leave some kind of scar, on the patient, their loved ones, or fellow victims.

Still, this doesn't let us off the hook for working hard, to know our craft, and to apply our best reasoning. It doesn't give us an excuse to be lazy or cavalier, or to put our wants above our patients' needs. Unfortunately that does happen. Doctors are people, too, and there are all kinds in the mix. But it's important to know what the priorities are, for everyone involved.

This page is blank so you can draw your own cartoon.

SJA '24

When They Leave You But They Won't Leave You Alone

"People who fight fire with fire usually end up with ashes."

—*Abigail Van Buren*

Those who ignore the past are doomed to repeat it. We've all heard it. It's an old adage, but the dusty cobwebs on its edges don't make it any less true. Unfortunately, there are people out there who seem unaware of it, or at the very least act as though it doesn't apply to them. The fact is that this is an axiom not just on the grand scale of international politics but for individuals as well, across the whole of human experience, good and bad.

It's very easy to feel that the circumstances that apply to us individually are unique. After all, we know all the intimate reasons of what happened to us and why. We didn't just have a front-row seat. We had an actual speaking part on the stage. Looking at everyone else, though, we're fortunate if we're any closer than the balcony, peering at the action through opera glasses and straining to catch every other word. But despite this feeling of singularity it's a truth that we are all strikingly similar in thoughts, feelings and reactions. The entire science of psychology is predicated on the fact that people do the same dumb things for the same dumb reasons they always have. Aristotle once complained about how the youth of his day 'think they know everything, and are always quite sure about it', as just one example. And despite being four centuries old, Shakespeare's plays still resonate.

Unfortunately, it's also a truth of human experience that relationships break down, sometimes quite dramatically... and bitterly. There can be a lot of leftover animosity that can develop into outright vindictiveness, where someone leaves you, but they won't leave you alone. While we can't control how other people act, we can do something about ourselves.

The problem with vindictiveness is that it causes pain and breeds resentment. Here's a little history lesson to illustrate: If you recall from your high school history classes, the First World War was caused by the assassination of

Archduke Franz Ferdinand of Austria. This may have been the single, easily identifiable event that set the wheels in motion, but the reality is much baser. The Great Powers of Europe had made a series of complicated alliances in the Balkans as the Ottoman Empire lost ground, and the political tension that erupted that summer of 1914 pulled in those Great Powers in much the same way a grade-school fistfight develops into a brawl involving older siblings, and then parents. If those Great Powers had had their wits about them the whole sorry affair could have been avoided. But each combatant looked across their borders and was afraid they saw their counterparts massing troops, so they did as well. Then the ones being watched, did their own watching, saw the *other* guy's troops, and built his up more. Overtures were made and warnings were issued to cease and desist *before* a war broke out, but you know what they say... actions speak louder than words, and when your neighbor is telling you that he will back down if you will, but he isn't....

To make things worse, this was the dawn of mechanized warfare and logistics depended heavily on rail systems with their fixed routes and complicated timetables. As divisions piled up on the borders, the need to keep everything coordinated – movement of personnel, food, ammunition, equipment, all coming from different places and at different times – essentially meant that, once things were under way it was nearly impossible to stop. To do so would throw each nation's entire movement schedules into chaos, bind up critical components in useless locations for weeks, cause unnecessary loss and waste, and could cost a victory before war had even begun. This, though, meant that every time the French looked at the Germans, or the Germans looked at the Russians, or the Russians looked at the Austrians, all they saw was more buildup. It was inevitable that someone would decide they weren't going to wait any longer and they (literally) pulled the trigger.

As it was, that was Germany.

The mayhem that followed has been exhaustively commented upon. Suffice it to say Germany was trounced in the end and Britain and France – the only two original combatants left standing – stuck it to Germany and forced them to pay the whole bill... and accept *all* the responsibility. Naturally the Germans felt they had been singled out and unfairly treated. After all, *everyone* had had their fingers in the Balkan pie. Maybe they were at fault, but they weren't the *only* ones at fault.

The conditions of the Armistice imposed by the victors led to the economic disaster of the Weimar Republic. This, coupled with the feelings of injustice, caused the resentment that directly led to the rise of nationalism and the Third Reich, and a second world war that was far, far worse than the first – at least in part because Hitler was able to remind Germany they had a score to settle. Now I'm not trying to justify in any way the actions of the Nazis. A million decisions were made on their own that led them down a very dark path. But the truth of the matter is, that if the Allies had shown a little restraint, there would not have been so much national angst for Hitler to draw upon and the Nazis would have been just another fringe political movement. A little, dare I say, compassion, and one of the worst tragedies of recorded history could have been avoided.

In contrast look at how things were handled the second time around. In 1945 it was the United States as the Last Man Standing. Instead of kicking Germany and Japan while they were down, we *built them up*. In Germany it was the Marshall Plan. In Japan it was the Dodge Program. Vast sums of money were poured into these people that, not long before, had been trying very, very hard to kill us (if you have any doubt about the teeth these 'beaten dogs' still had in them even at the very end, read about the battles of Berlin and Okinawa). Now, lest you think that this was the population of the Great Ol' US of A being generous and forgiving, I'd just like to point out that even twenty years later as a small child I still heard people complaining bitterly and often about how we were 'giving all our money to foreigners'. And yet now these countries are economic powerhouses and two of our staunchest allies (even more so than France and the UK).

As I noted above, what's true on the grand scale is often true in the microcosms of our lives. The point is that if you're being kicked while you're down, don't let it consume you to the point you only think about 'getting your due' and you wind up being more of an S.O.B. than the guy that started it. Do what you need to protect yourself, and then hold up. If you're the one doing the kicking, watch yourself – you may just end up creating a monster.

This page is blank because I needed an even number of pages for the printer

Forgiveness—But How?

"Everyone says that forgiveness is a lovely
idea until he has something to forgive."
—*Henry Wadsworth Longfellow*

Forgiveness is something that I know, at least for myself, I've struggled with, and I'm sure many of you
have as well. There's nothing wrong with the fact that
you've struggled, it's a really important, and yet really difficult principle. And *I* know it's important, and I know *why*
it's important. I've seen the wonderful things that can happen when you *do* forgive . . .

But it's the nuts-and-bolts of making it happen that's
the hard part. And that's what I want to talk about.

But first, a little groundwork. What is 'forgiveness'?

The popular idea of forgiveness is usually encapsulated in the snippet 'forgive and forget'. This dime-store psychology implies that, sooner or later, you should just put everything behind you, and get back to a point in your relationship with the person that hurt you, to when you were chums. That may be an achievable goal if you're only mad at your BFF for roasting you on the group chat.

But what if that person is your abuser? What if they have done so much damage to you, or those you love, that you will be years sweeping up the pieces of a shattered soul and trying to figure out why you shouldn't just chuck it all in the dustbin? If you will be needing professional help to deal with the fallout? What if this person has figuratively, or literally, burned you alive?

What if they've made you wish you were dead?

I'd like to take a moment to review what's actually expected of us. No matter our moral system, by and large we are encouraged to forgive as many times as someone asks it of us, and is genuinely repentant. However, if they are not, and they pose a real threat to our welfare, we are allowed to defend ourselves. After all, if they take your coat, you should be willing to give them your cloak, but there is nothing said about handing over your shirt and your shoes as well. (A thoughtful and knowledgeable friend of mine once pointed out that in ancient Jewish culture, the shame of seeing someone naked was on the beholder, not the person with no clothing. So to give someone the rest of your clothes was actually forcing them to acknowledge the shame of your destitution *that they caused*, and was in fact a form of passive resistance.)

So forgive as often as forgiveness is asked, but protect yourself. We are expected to forgive those who ask it of us, but the other person must put something into it – they must be asking with repentance and real intent. We're better off giving them the benefit of the doubt if we're not certain of their sincerity, but in any case we are *not* required to put ourselves in harm's way again indefinitely.

But what about to the process of forgiveness? How do we actually make this work? I want to explain this with a metaphor, and I'm going to use a debt of money.

You make someone a loan. They have now received something of yours, that wasn't theirs. Eventually you want payment made on that loan. You want your money back.

What payment do we want made on an *offense*?

We want . . . revenge.

We want to see them suffer.

We want them to feel our pain.

That's really it, isn't it?

If you forgive a monetary debt, you no longer require the money to be returned. You don't require that pound of silver. In like fashion, when you forgive an offense, you no longer expect to get back that pound of flesh.

You no longer desire, or at least expect, to watch the other person suffer. We aren't supposed to seek the misfortune of another, and desiring to see them suffer falls under that.

Training yourself to forgo wishing suffering onto another person, even if, or *especially if*, they deserve it, makes *you* a better person.

What about forgetting? This, I think, is really the hardest part. Once a trust has been broken it's very difficult to rebuild it. My question is, is it really necessary to rebuild that trust? Can you ever hang out like buddies again?

Should you?

When a monetary debt is forgiven, the payment is written off. But the record of the unpaid debt remains. Only when it is removed from that credit report is it officially forgotten. But even so the credit *score* will still be in the tank until the debtor can prove they can responsibly handle a new debt. But *that* is on the shoulders of the debtor, and it is *their* burden to convince someone to give them a new debt with which to prove themselves.

We, as the people whose forgiveness is sought after, are like the credit reporting agencies. If we forget the debt, we take it off their 'report'.

We don't remind them of it. We don't throw it up in their face every time we see them. We don't gripe to other people about it, or make suggestive hints to others about their past mistakes.

There is an obvious exception to that last, if the person is a real, predatory threat to those who don't know them, where failing to warn another person away would put them at risk. But in most circumstances, if one of our friends asks why we don't associate with the offender any more, and keeping the situation quiet would do our friend no harm, there is really no reason to air old dirty laundry.

The offender's credit with us may not be very good, and it may take a long time for them – *for them* – to change that, if they ever do, but *we* are no longer keeping score on what they've done.

But there is nothing that says you have to make them a new loan, that you have to put yourself in that position again.

Unfortunately our culture has distorted the truth of this very important principle. Well-meaning folks toss off that phrase to 'forgive and forget', and don't give you any context or practical advice, which leaves you feeling somehow inadequate when you can't do that. Now don't get me wrong, it's good if you can actually forgive, and forget, and be buds again. But sometimes that isn't achievable. Sometimes the wounds are too deep.

Now I am not here to let you off the hook for trying to reconcile. That is *always* the goal. It would be a truly wonderful world if we really could put all our past hurts behind us. But human lives are messy, and sometimes people exercise their own agency to the severe harm of others.

In order to put your own soul at peace, what you need to do in a nutshell, is, first, stop seeking the other person's suffering, and second, stop talking it up.

If that's all you can manage, start with that. Then see how far you can get from there.

In any case do not, under any circumstances, think there is something wrong with you because you can't bring yourself to take a seat on the park bench next to that person who abused you. Even if it is all you can do, to accomplish these two things I mentioned, then you *can* hold your head up.

;

"...used when an author could've chosen to end their sentence, but chose not to. The author is you and the sentence is your life."

—*Amy Bleuel*

I've been through a lot of transitions in my life. Some have been good: going from living with parents to being a homeowner, from being a newlywed to being a father, or making the NCO ranks in the Army. Some have been extremely challenging, though no less voluntary: embarking on that military journey in my thirties, switching from blue-collar buckaroo to college student and eventually to physician. And some have been thrust upon me and decidedly unpleasant. But one thing I can tell you is that, as far as I'm concerned, transitions always *suck*.

. **;** .

I'm the kind of guy that likes to stay in a rut once I've found it. Uncertainty gives me what my grandma used to call 'conniptions' (not so much the rage part, mostly the hysterics, at least on the inside). It seems that, no matter how hard I work at making things as smooth as possible, there's always something coming out of left field that I didn't anticipate, or someone upon whom I was depending, who dropped the ball at an inopportune time and then I'm left scrambling. And sometimes it's me dropping that ball, and it careens downhill taking out everything in its path. Thankfully joining the Army was one of my earlier transitions and my experiences there gave me a sound piece of advice:

Adapt. Improvise. Overcome.

The Marines have a similar, though decidedly more succinct expression: *Semper Gumby*, 'always flexible', referencing a kids' show that I used to watch growing up and with which I've now dated myself. Yeah, I'm that old. It's good advice, though. We've won two world wars thinking on our feet. A Russian strategist once famously commented "One of the serious problems in planning against American doctrine is that the Americans do not read their manuals nor do they feel any obligation to follow their doctrine". And in a typically American fashion, is one of Murphy's Laws of Combat: "Professional soldiers are predictable but the world is full of dangerous amateurs". (There are a lot of gems in Murphy's Laws of Combat. If you've never read them, I encourage you to look them up.)

As I said a couple paragraphs ago, sometimes those transitions are good, and sometimes they're just... not. Sometimes you've literally bet the farm, and lost. Then what? The world is full of pithy sayings to help you keep your chin up through failure, like the one that inspired the title of this book, by John Sinclair: *Failure is a bruise, not a tattoo*. Some other good ones I've heard are, *When you feel you've been buried, maybe you've been planted. Bloom!* Or, *If you're going through Hell, keep going!* I'm sure you could think of several more, all offered by well-meaning folks that are trying to make you feel better about finding yourself in the midst of a crapshow. And that's good, and you should thank those folks for caring, because a lot of people don't.

But I'm not going to tell you everything is going to be okay. There's no way to know that for sure and you and I both know that. Sometimes you just don't even have a broom to sweep up the shards, never mind glue to put them back into some semblance of what they once were. But what I can tell you is that Mr. Sinclair had it right. Your successes you can usually frame and hang on your 'love-me wall' for the rest of Time and *failure is only a bruise*. It will heal. You will get through it, somehow, some way, though probably not in a way you'd expect. Sometimes those ill winds bring a kite with them! There will come a day when you find yourself on the other side of those deep waters – even if the current took you way further downstream than you wanted. And you *will* lose things along the way, because experience doesn't come cheap (here's another one, an old Chinese proverb: *"In the course of a long and successful life a man must be prepared to abandon his baggage several times"*). What you have to do, is keep going, and don't be too proud to ask for help. Get up one more time than you fell down, even if you have to grab onto someone else's hand to do it. There are a lot of really great people all around you who've done that already that you don't even know about. *Go find them.*

And finally, here's another gem from my days in the Armored Cav: *The best way out of an ambush, is through it.*

Semper Gumby, my friends.

Footnotes

Babies And Bathwater

1. Dowell D, Haegerich TM, Chou R. CDC Guideline for Prescribing Opioids for Chronic Pain — United States, 2016. MMWR Recomm Rep 2016;65(No. RR-1):1–49. DOI: http://dx.doi.org/10.15585/mmwr.rr6501e1.

2. Chen, C., Pettersson, E., Summit, A.G. et al. Chronic pain conditions and risk of suicidal behavior: a 10-year longitudinal co-twin control study. BMC Med 21, 9 (2023). https://doi.org/10.1186/s12916-022-02703-8

3. Harm Reduction Ohio. 2022, October 17. First Projection of 2022: Overdose deaths on track to decline this year. https://www.harmreductionohio.org/overdose-death-on-track-to-decline-lightly-in-2022/

4. National Institute on Drug Abuse. 2023, June 30. Drug Overdose Death Rates. https://nida.nih.gov/research-topics/trends-statistics/overdose-death-rates#:~:text=Opioid-involved%20overdose%20deaths%20rose%20from%2021%2C089%20in%202010,again%20in%202021%20with%2080%2C411%20reported%20overdose%20deaths.

5. CDC Media Relations. 2019, April 24. CDC Advises Against Misapplication of the Guideline for Prescribing Opioids for Chronic Pain [Press Release]. https://archive.cdc.gov/#/details?url=https://www.cdc.gov/media/releases/2019/s0424-advises-misapplication-guideline-prescribing-opioids.html

Damned If We Do, Damned If We Don't?

1.   CDC (n.d.). *Understanding the Opioid Overdose Epidemic*. Centers for Disease Control and Prevention. Retrieved March 24, 2024, from https://www.cdc.gov/opioids/basics/epidemic.html#:~:text=The%20first%20wave%20began%20with%20increased%20prescribing%20of,rapid%20increases%20in%20overdose%20deaths%20involving%20heroin%204.

2.   Dowell D, Haegerich TM, Chou R. CDC Guideline for Prescribing Opioids for Chronic Pain — United States, 2016. MMWR Recomm Rep 2016;65(No. RR-1):1–49. DOI: http://dx.doi.org/10.15585/mmwr.rr6501e1.

3.   Kennedy MC, Crabtree A, Nolan S, Mok WY, Cui Z, Chong M, et al. (2022) Discontinuation and tapering of prescribed opioids and risk of overdose among people on long-term opioid therapy for pain with and without opioid use disorder in British Columbia, Canada: A retrospective cohort study. PLoS Med 19(12): e1004123. https://doi.org/10.1371/journal.pmed.1004123

4.   Harm Reduction Ohio (2024, March 8). *Ohio overdose deaths decline about 6% in 2023*. Retrieved March 25, 2024, from https://www.harmreductionohio.org/ohio-overdose-deaths-decline-in-2023/

5.   Anson, P. (2022, December 13). *DEA Finalizes Cuts in 2023 Opioid Supply*. Pain News Network. Retrieved March 24, 2024, from https://www.painnewsnetwork.org/stories/2022/12/13/dea-finalizes-cuts-in-2023-opioid-supply

6.   Anson, P. (2023, November 3). *DEA Plans Further Cuts in Rx Opioid Supply in 2024*. Retrieved March 24, 2024, from https://www.painnewsnetwork.org/stories/2023/11/3/dea-plans-further-cuts-in-rx-opioid-supply-in-2024

7.   Anson, P. (2023, October 16). *Drug and Medical Supply Shortages Impacting Patient Safety at 'Alarming Rate'*. Retrieved March 25,

2024, from https://www.painnewsnetwork.org/sto-ries/2023/10/16/drug-and-medical-supply-shortages-impacting-pa-tient-safety-at-alarming-rate

8.   Dodge, B. (2019, October 14). *DEA Says It Doesn't 'Regulate Practice of Medicine' Amid Patient Backlash to Proposed Opioid Pre-scription Cuts*. Retrieved March 25, 2024, from https://www.newsweek.com/dea-responds-chronic-pain-victims-opi-oid-prescriptions-1465090

9.   Anson, P. (2023, October 9). *Lawsuits Accuse DEA of 'Incompe-tence' in Regulating Drug Supply*. Retrieved March 25, 2024, from https://www.painnewsnetwork.org/stories/2023/10/9/lawsuits-ac-cuse-dea-of-incompetence-in-regulating-drug-supply

10.   United States Drug Enforcement Administration (2022, March 23). *DEA's Commitment to Expanding Access to Medication-Assisted Treatment*. DEA. Retrieved March 25, 2024, from https://www.dea.gov/press-releases/2022/03/23/deas-commitment-expanding-access-medication-assisted-treatment

11.   Centers for Disease Control and Prevention (2019, April 24). *CDC Advises Against Misapplication of the Guideline for Prescribing Opioids for Chronic Pain*. CDC. Retrieved March 25, 2024, from https://archive.cdc.gov/#/details?url=https://www.cdc.gov/me-dia/releases/2019/s0424-advises-misapplication-guideline-prescribing-opioids.html

12.   Stone, W., & Huang, P. (2022, November 3). *CDC issues new opi-oid prescribing guidance, giving doctors more leeway to treat pain*. GBH: What Matters To You. Retrieved March 25, 2024, from https://archive.cdc.gov/#/details?url=https://www.cdc.gov/me-dia/releases/2019/s0424-advises-misapplication-guideline-prescribing-opioids.html

13.   Centers for Disease Control and Prevention (2022, November 3). *Summary of the 2022 Clinical Practice Guideline for Prescribing Opi-oids for Pain*. CDC. Retrieved March 25, 2024, from https://www.cdc.gov/opioids/patients/guideline.html

Why I No Longer Practice Medicine In Ohio

1.   Dowell D, Haegerich T, Chou R. 2016, March 15. *CDC Guidelines for Prescribing Opioids for Chronic Pain – United States, 2016.* MMWR Recomm Rep 2016;65(No. RR6501e1er) (pp 1-50). https://www.cdc.gov/media/modules/dpk/2016/dpk-pod/rr6501e1er-ebook.pdf

2.   CDC Media Relations. 2019, April 24. *CDC Advises Against Misapplication of the Guideline for Prescribing Opioids for Chronic Pain [Press Release].* https://archive.cdc.gov/#/details?url=https://www.cdc.gov/media/releases/2019/s0424-advises-misapplication-guideline-prescribing-opioids.html

3.   Harm Reduction Ohio. 2022, October 17. *First Projection of 2022: Overdose deaths on track to decline this year.* https://www.harmreductionohio.org/overdose-death-on-track-to-decline-lightly-in-2022/

4.   Powell, Alvin. 2022, November 21. *New CDC guidelines a 'corrective' for opioid prescriptions, specialist says.* The Harvard Gazette. https://news.harvard.edu/gazette/story/2022/11/new-cdc-guidelines-a-corrective-for-opioid-prescriptions-specialist-says/

5.   Kennedy M, Crabtree A, Nolan S, et al. 2022, December 1. *Discontinuation and tapering of prescribed opioids and risk of overdose among people on long-term opioid therapy for pain with and without opioid use disorder in British Columbia: a retrospective cohort study.* PLOS Medicine. https://journals.plos.org/plosmedicine/article?id=10.1371/journal.pmed.1004123

6.   fd.org (2022, June 27). *SCOTUS Unanimously Rules In Favor Of Doctors In Pill Mill Case.* Fd.org Defender Services Office, Training Division from https://www.fd.org/news/scotus-unanimously-rules-favor-doctors-pill-mill-case

About The Author

Steve grew up on a farm in Northeast Ohio, then worked in factories for fifteen years before going back to school and becoming a physician. His other writing ventures have been novels, and he has won awards for his writing in collaboration with Michael Eging on *The Silver Horn Echoes: A Song of Roland*, and *The Paladin of Shadow Chronicles: Book One, Annwyn's Blood*, and *Book Two: Ash and Ruin*.

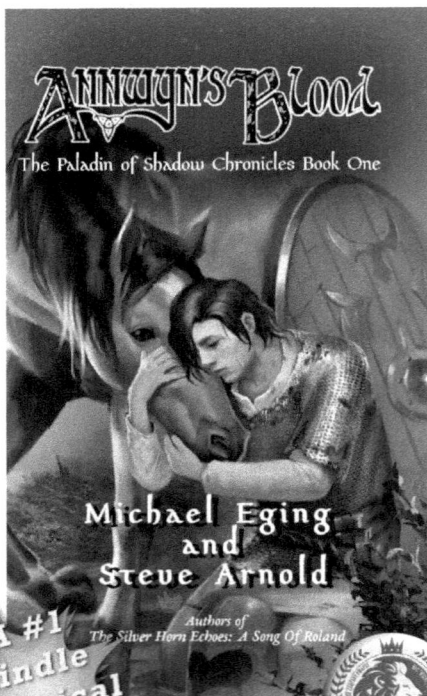